Record of experiments at Des Lignes sugar experiment station, Baldwin, La., during the season of 1888

Charles Albert Crampton

U. S. DEPARTMENT OF AGRICULTURE.

DIVISION OF CHEMISTRY.

BULLETIN   No. 22.

RECORD OF EXPERIMENTS

AT

DES LIGNES SUGAR EXPERIMENT STATION,

BALDWIN, LA.,

DURING THE SEASON OF 1888.

BY

C. A. CRAMPTON,

ASSISTANT CHEMIST.

PUBLISHED BY AUTHORITY OF THE SECRETARY OF AGRICULTURE.

WASHINGTON:
GOVERNMENT PRINTING OFFICE.
1889.

U. S. DEPARTMENT OF AGRICULTURE.
DIVISION OF CHEMISTRY.

BULLETIN   No. 22.

RECORD OF EXPERIMENTS

AT

DES LIGNES SUGAR EXPERIMENT STATION,

BALDWIN, LA.,

DURING THE SEASON OF 1888.

BY

C. A. CRAMPTON,
ASSISTANT CHEMIST.

PUBLISHED BY AUTHORITY OF THE SECRETARY OF AGRICULTURE.

WASHINGTON:
GOVERNMENT PRINTING OFFICE.
1889.

PREFATORY NOTE.

SIR: I beg to place before you for your inspection and approval the report of Dr. C. A. Crampton, containing the data collected at the Des Lignes Plantation of Shattuck & Hoffman during the manufacturing season of 1888.

Although the manufacturing results were favorable, the proprietors of this plantation have decided to displace their roller mills and substitute therefor a diffusion battery. The data herein contained will be found of value especially by those planters who contemplate changing from milling to diffusion.

Respectfully,

H. W. WILEY,
Chemist.

Hon. J. M. RUSK,
Secretary of Agriculture.

3

LETTER OF SUBMITTAL.

SIR: I have the honor to submit herewith my report on the work done at the Des Lignes Sugar Experiment Station during the season of 1888.
Respectfully,

C. A. CRAMPTON,
Assistant Chemist.

Dr. H. W. WILEY,
Chemist.

5

EXPERIMENTS AT DES LIGNES SUGAR EXPERIMENT STATION, BALDWIN, LA.

The grinding season of 1888 was commenced at Des Lignes plantation on October 8, and finished November 30. I had expected to be at the station by the middle of October, but was detained in Kansas, partly by the work on sorghum at the Sterling Experiment Station, and partly by work in connection with an exhibit illustrative of the sorghum-sugar industry to be sent to the Paris Exposition as a part of the Department's exhibit there. In consequence of this delay I did not arrive at Des Lignes until the 1st of November. The chemical control of the mill was begun November 5, and continued until the close of the season, extending over a period of four weeks, or just one-half the manufacturing season. In addition to the careful control of the operation of the sugar-house during this period, several lines of experiment were carried on, and while the limited time for observation and the stress of work necessarily prevented my giving these experiments anything like the amount of care and attention I could have wished, yet some results were obtained that may be worth recording, if for no other purpose than to call more general attention to the necessity of more extended work in the same directions.

The lack of sufficient time will serve as an apology, I hope, for the scantiness of the data in the experimental work, and for the unsolved problems in connection with some of the sources of loss.

Every facility possible was extended me by Messrs. Shattuck & Hoffman, the proprietors of the plantation, in furtherance of experiments likely to prove of benefit to the industry at large, and my thanks are due to them, and also to Mr. C. P. Binnings, their manager, to whom I am under great obligations for his intelligent aid, to say nothing of personal courtesies.

EQUIPMENT OF THE FACTORY.

The extraction was performed by a six-roller mill, composed of two three-roller mills set tandem. Each mill was driven by separate engines. The diameter of the rolls was 27 inches, length, 4 feet. The second mill was provided with an hydraulic regulator. Maceration was practiced all through the season, the water being added from a rose placed above the intermediate carrier. The juice was sulphured and clarified in the usual way, and evaporated in a double effect Rillieux pan, one of the original pattern. It had horizontal tubes of about 1,225 square feet heating surface. Two 7½-foot strike pans were used in reducing the sirup to massecuite. For pressing the scums two Niles filter presses were used, of 220 square feet of filtering surface each. These were not adequate to the work, however, and a good proportion of the skimmings was settled and reclarified.

A machine for automatically weighing the juice was constructed at the beginning of the season by Mr. A. R. Shattuck, upon his own designs, and at considerable expense. Its operation did not prove satisfactory, however, and when I reached the plantation it had been laid aside.

OPERATION OF THE FACTORY BY WEEKLY PERIODS.

It has been the custom at this plantation to keep each week's running of the factory separate. The mill is shut down every Sunday, all the sirup on hand boiled up, the first and second sugar barreled and weighed, and wagon sugar estimated. Similarly the amount of cane ground during the week is kept, and if any is left on the yard over Sunday the quantity is estimated and charged to the following week. Such a system is somewhat difficult to carry out practically, and would doubtless be still more so in a larger house, but the checking of the operations of the factory is much facilitated by it, and an opportunity afforded for making comparisons that would be difficult to obtain otherwise. For comparing the results of one week's run with another during the season the third sugars were estimated, as indicated above, but the wagons were all marked and kept separate, and when they were run off this spring the exact amount of third sugar and molasses was ascertained for each week, thus completing the statistics. Following the same plan, the analyses for each week were kept separate, this being an easy matter, of course, and in the tables results are given by weekly runs.

QUALITY OF SUGAR.

"Yellow clarified" first sugars were made, and what are known as "cut seconds," that is a portion of first massecuite, is left in the pan to serve as a grain for the seconds. This is quite a favorite method of boiling in Louisiana. Its advisability is somewhat questionable from a scientific point of view, as it sacrifices a part of the first sugar and subjects it to a second boiling. It must therefore diminish the yield to some extent; but on the other hand it increases the proportion of high grade product so that a great many conditions of price, etc., are brought into the problem and I have made no attempt to solve it. The molasses from seconds was boiled to string proof, and allowed to stand until granulated.

CHEMICAL CONTROL.

The following tables show the daily analyses of the various products for the four weeks during which the house was under chemical control. I consider the sulphured juice as it went into the clarifiers as a starting point for this control since this was the first point at which accurate gauging could be made. Analyses are given of the mixed juice as it came from the mill, but the difficulties in the way of securing an accurate sampling of a continuous stream of juice, especially when the cane varied so much as it did at Des Lignes, prevents any comparison of this product with those following it. During the first week the mill juices were taken with the maceration water added, just as they came from the mill. After that the water was turned off while the samples were being taken.

The average analyses for each week, with the sugars and molasses, are summarized in the following tables:

Table showing summary by weeks.

FIFTH WEEK.

Product.	No. of analyses.	Total solids.	Sucrose.	Glucose.	Coefficient of purity.	Glucose per cent. sucrose.
		Per cent.	*Per cent.*	*Per cent.*		
Mill juice..........	6	15.04	12.35	1.48	82.1	11.98*
Sulphured juice....	6	15.23	12.45	1.47	81.7	11.80
Clarified juice	6	15.77	12.99	1.48	82.4	11.39
Sirup	3	40.16	32.54	4.15	81.2	12.71
First massecuite ..	3	....	74.85	9.84	....	13.15
First sugar	3	....	98.47	.....	.....	.....
Second sugar......	2	....	97.30	.....	.....	.....
Third sugar	1	....	89.60	.....	.....	.....
Third molasses	1	65.52	27.64	30.10	42.18	108.90

* With maceration water added between mills.

SIXTH WEEK.

Product.	No. of analyses.	Total solids.	Sucrose.	Glucose.	Coefficient of purity.	Glucose per cent. sucrose.
Mill juice............	11	15.86	13.72	1.06	86.5	7.72
Sulphured juice ...	5	15.24	12.83	1.05	84.1	8.18
Clarified juice	5	15.52	13.10	1.09	84.4	8.32
Sirup	3	44.09	36.73	3.63	83.3	9.80
First massecuite ..	3	....	76.33	8.09	.....	10.60
First sugar	1	....	97.80	.....	.....	.....
Second sugar	1	....	97.40	.....	.....	.....
Third sugar	1	....	90.40	.....	.....	.....
Third molasses	1	70.75	41.24	21.94	58.29	53.20

Table showing summary by weeks—Continued.

SEVENTH WEEK.

Mill juice..........	8	15.65	13.65	.96	87.2	7.03
Sulphured juice....	11	14.81	12.72	.95	85.9	7.47
Clarified juice	6	15.31	13.01	.98	85.0	7.53
Sirup..............	5	39.22	32.90	2.96	83.8	9.00
First massecuite ..	5	....	77.98	7.48	....	9.59
First sugar	1	....	98.50	....	....	....
Second sugar	1	....	98.30	....	....	....
Third sugar........	1	....	87.00	....	....	....
Third molasses	1	69.58	38.68	23.14	55.59	59.82

EIGHTH WEEK.

Mill juice..........	5	15.90	14.14	.83	88.9	5.87
Sulphured juice....	12	14.83	13.00	.79	87.6	6.08
Clarified juice......	5	15.19	13.34	.82	87.8	6.15
Sirup........	8	38.40	32.34	2.48	84.1	7.67
First massecuite ..	8	....	79.70	6.21	....	7.79
First sugar	1	....	98.90	....	....	....
Second sugar	1	....	98.50	....	....	....
Third sugar........	1	....	90.20	....	....	....
Third molasses	1	72.20	40.22	23.98	55.71	59.62

AVERAGE FOR FOUR WEEKS.

Product.	Total solids.	Sucrose.	Glucose.	Coefficient of purity.	Glucose per cent. sucrose.
	Per cent.	*Per cent.*	*Per cent.*		
Mill juice	15.80	13.84	.95	87.6	8.15
Sulphured juice	15.03	12.70	1.06	84.8	8.38
Clarified juice	15.36	13.11	1.09	84.9	8.35
Sirup......................	40.47	33.63	3.30	83.1	9.79
First massecuite	....	77.21	7.90	....	10.28
First sugar................	....	98.42	....	....	....
Second sugar..............	....	97.88	....	....	....
Third sugar	....	89.30	....	....	....
Third molasses............	69.51	36.95	24.79	52.94	70.37

Table of daily analyses.

Fifth week's run, November 5 to November 10, inclusive.

	No.	Date.	Solids.	Sucrose.	Glucose.
			Per cent.	*Per cent*	*Per cent.*
Mill juice......................	10	Nov. 5	14.98	12.15	1.54*
	21	Nov. 6	15.50	12.71	1.38*
	28	Nov. 7	15.58	12.41	1.70*
	35	Nov. 8	14.68	12.27	1.53*
	49	Nov. 9	15.00	12.35	Lost. *
	61	Nov. 10	14.50	12.20	1.26*
Average	......	....	15.04	12.35	1.48
Coefficient of purity........	......	....	....	....	82.10
Glucose per cent. sucrose ..	......	....	....	....	11.98
Sulphured juices	11	Nov. 5	15.08	12.39	1.48
	22	Nov. 6	15.45	12.73	1.39
	29	Nov. 7	15.60	12.33	1.71
	38	Nov. 8	14.90	12.31	1.58
	52	Nov. 9	15.24	12.62	1.35
	64	Nov. 10	14.91	12.33	1.30
Average	......	....	15.23	12.45	1.47
Coefficient of purity........	......	....	....	....	81.70
Glucose per cent. sucrose ..	......	....	....	....	11.80
Clarified juices..............	12	Nov. 5	15.85	13.25	1.49
	23	Nov. 6	15.95	13.25	1.43
	30	Nov. 7	16.50	13.36	1.72
	39	Nov. 8	15.60	12.68	1.50
	53	Nov. 9	15.50	12.80	1.38
	68	Nov. 10	15.20	12.63	1.37
Average	....	....	15.77	12.99	1.48
Coefficient of purity........	......	....	....	....	82.40
Glucose per cent. sucrose ..	......	....	....	....	11.39
Sirup	32	Nov. 7	40.49	33.20	4.55
	34	Nov. 7	44.77	35.10	4.67
	45	Nov. 8	40.15	32.85	4.06
	48	Nov. 9	35.25	29.60	3.33
Average	......	....	40.16	32.54	4.15
Coefficient of purity........	......	....	....	....	81.20
Glucose per cent. sucrose ..	......	....	....	....	12.71
First masscuite............	26	Nov. 7	....	74.60	10.20
	27	Nov. 7	....	74.40	10.10
	46	Nov. 8	....	75.40	9.80
	47	Nov. 9	....	75.00	9.26
Average	......	....	....	74.85	9.84
Glucose per cent. sucrose ..	......	....	....	....	13.15

* With maceration water added.

Table of daily analyses—Continued.

Sixth week's run, November 13 to November 17, inclusive.

	No.	Date.	Solids.	Sucrose.	Glucose.
			Per cent.	*Per cent.*	*Per cent.*
Mill juice......................	82	Nov. 13	15.30	12.85	1.26
	87	Nov. 13	15.58	12.90	1.33
	92	Nov. 14	15.76	13.37	1.22
	94	Nov. 14	15.46	13.34	1.09
	102	Nov. 15	16.07	13.78	1.09
	109	Nov. 15	15.51	13.43	1.09
	118	Nov. 16	17.33	15.85	.62
	122	Nov. 16	15.53	13.57	1.08
	132	Nov. 17	16.20	14.32	.91
	140	Nov. 17	15.87	13.82	.94
Average			15.86	13.72	1.06
Coefficient of purity........					86.50
Glucose per cent. sucrose ..					7.72
Sulphured juices..............	84	Nov. 13	14.88	12.25	1.20
	97	Nov. 14	15.01	12.64	1.13
	105	Nov. 15	15.18	12.43	1.06
	123	Nov. 16	15.61	13.49	.93
	133	Nov. 17	15.50	13.35	.95
Average			15.24	12.83	1.05
Coefficient of purity........					84.10
Glucose per cent. sucrose ..					8.18
Clarified juices..............	85	Nov. 13	15.16	12.63	1.21
	98	Nov. 14	15.41	13.01	1.10
	107	Nov. 15	15.48	13.15	1.10
	125	Nov. 16	15.71	13.24	1.04
	135	Nov. 17	15.84	13.48	1.01
Average			15.52	13.10	1.09
Coefficient of purity........					84.40
Glucose per cent. sucrose ..					8.32
Sirup	77	Nov. 13	41.24	34.40	3.52
	95	Nov. 14	46.40	38.40	3.62
	112	Nov. 15	44.63	37.40	3.76
Average			44.09	36.73	3.63
Coefficient of purity........					83.30
Glucose per cent. sucrose ..					9.80
First massecuite..............	78	Nov. 13		75.20	8.33
	96	Nov. 14		77.80	8.00
	113	Nov. 15		76.00	7.93
Average				76.33	8.09
Glucose per cent. sucrose ..					10.60

Table of daily analyses—Continued.

Seventh week's run, November 19 to November 24, inclusive.

	No.	Date.	Solids.	Sucrose.	Glucose.
			Per cent.	*Per cent.*	*Per cent.*
Mill juices......................	143	Nov. 19	16.01	13.71	1.20
	146	Nov. 19	15.94	13.80	1.01
	155	Nov. 20	15.50	13.37	1.12
	166	Nov. 21	14.80	12.97	.96
	169	Nov. 21	15.20	13.24	.98
	179	Nov. 22	15.50	13.08	1.02
	193	Nov. 23	15.47	13.67	.86
	205	Nov. 24	16.77	15.40	.55
Average......................	......	....	15.65	13.65	.96
Coefficient of purity........	......	....	....	....	87.20
Glucose per cent. sucrose...	......	....	....	... .	7.03
Sulphured juices	144	Nov. 19	15.20	12.83	1.10
	151	Nov. 19	15.06	12.49	1.16
	158	Nov. 20	14.64	12.51	1.00
	164	Nov. 20	14.80	12.70	.99
	172	Nov. 21	14.76	12.59	.93
	182	Nov. 22	14.58	12.31	1.00
	189	Nov. 22	14.66	12.99	.90
	196	Nov. 23	14.94	13.03	.89
	203	Nov. 23	14.88	12.74	.91
	206	Nov. 24	14.96	13.22	.80
	213	Nov. 24	14.44	12.47	.82
Average......................	......	....	14.81	12.72	.95
Coefficient of purity........	......	....	....	....	85.90
Glucose per cent. sucrose...	......	....	....	....	7.47
Clarified juices	147	Nov. 19	15.80	13.34	1.11
	160	Nov. 20	15.14	12.73	1.05
	174	Nov. 21	15.30	12.97	.92
	184	Nov. 22	14.84	12.54	1.03
	198	Nov. 23	15.37	13.20	.94
	208	Nov. 24	15.44	13.29	.8
Average......................	......	....	15.31	13.01	.98
Coefficient of purity	......	....	....	....	85.00
Glucose per cent. sucrose...	......	....	.. ..	....	7.53
Sirup	161	Nov. 20	44.30	36.10	3.33
	175	Nov. 21	43.07	36.50	3.52
	187	Nov. 22	38.80	33.20	3.03
	209	Nov. 24	34.57	29.80	2.59
	211	Nov. 24	33.35	28.90	2.35
Average......................	......	....	39.22	32.90	2.96
Coefficient of purity	......	....	....	....	83.90
Glucose per cent. sucrose...	......	....	....	....	9.00
First massecuite	162	Nov. 20	....	77.40	7.52
	176	Nov. 21	....	77.20	8.20
	188	Nov. 22	....	79.20	7.76
	210	Nov. 24	....	77.40	6.90
	212	Nov. 24	....	78.10	7.04
Average......................	......	....	....	77.96	7.48
Glucose per cent. sucrose...	......	....	....	....	9.59

Table of daily analyses—Continued.

Eighth week's run, November 26 to November 30, inclusive.

	No.	Date.	Solids.	Sucrose.	Glucose.
			Per cent.	*Per cent.*	*Per cent.*
Mill juices	218	Nov. 26	15.90	13.98	.93
	239	Nov. 27	15.37	13.62	.87
	257	Nov. 28	15.76	13.98	.81
	273	Nov. 29	16.01	14.36	.71
	285	Nov. 30	16.48	14.78	.81
Average			15.90	14.14	.83
Coefficient of purity					88.90
Glucose per cent. sucrose					5.87
Sulphured juices	221	Nov. 26	14.81	12.99	.89
	242	Nov. 27	14.76	12.78	.87
	260	Nov. 28	14.63	12.78	.86
	266	Nov. 28	14.68	12.60	.85
	276	Nov. 29	14.82	13.31	.67
	282	Nov. 29	14.89	13.23	.71
	288	Nov. 30	14.80	13.22	.73
	298	Nov. 30	15.24	13.11	.71
Average			14.83	13.00	.79
Coefficient of purity					87.60
Glucose per cent. sucrose					6.08
Clarified juices	222	Nov. 26	14.81	12.69	.89
	243	Nov. 27	15.38	13.21	.88
	261	Nov. 28	15.31	13.45	.81
	277	Nov. 29	15.20	13.97	.80
	289	Nov. 30	15.24	13.40	.74
Average			15.19	13.34	.82
Coefficient of purity					87.80
Glucose per cent. sucrose					6.15
Sirup	244	Nov. 27	38.57	32.60	3.18
	246	Nov. 27	40.75	34.90	3.22
	252	Nov. 27	32.80	28.80	2.22
	267	Nov. 28	33.47	29.60	2.18
	269	Nov. 29	37.60	32.70	2.36
	279	Nov. 29	36.48	31.80	2.24
	283	Nov. 30	51.16	36.00	2.47
	299	Nov. 30	36.40	32.30	1.96
Average			38.40	32.34	2.48
Coefficient of purity					84.10
Glucose per cent. sucrose					7.67
First massecuite	245	Nov. 27		78.50	7.70
	247	Nov. 27		78.80	6.90
	253	Nov. 27		78.80	6.94
	268	Nov. 28		79.90	6.17
	270	Nov. 29		80.50	5.86
	280	Nov. 29		79.40	5.58
	284	Nov. 30		81.00	5.50
	300	Nov. 30		80.70	5.00
Average				79.70	6.21
Glucose per cent. sucrose					7.79

The samples of mill juice were taken during the fifth week, with the water of maceration added. After that time this water was turned off when the sample was being taken, so as to obtain the normal juice of the cane as nearly as possible. Owing to the difficulty of obtaining accurate samples from a continuous stream of juice, however, these samples of mill juice can not properly be compared with later products, and are of value simply as showing the quality of cane going into the house. I began control work with the sulphured juice, taking this as a starting point, as accurate samples of it could be obtained, which properly represented the juice as it entered the house. For an exact comparison of the sulphured and clarified juices, the corresponding samples of each, in parallel lines, should be taken, and if this is done it will be seen that little or no increase in the purity was attained by the process of clarification contrary to the usual experience, the removal of solids in the scums usually raising the coefficient of purity one or two points.

MANUFACTURING DATA.

The manufacturing data for the entire season may be given briefly as follows:

Cane grown ....tons.. 8,635

Merchantable sugar made:
First ....pounds.. 698,064
Second...do.... 346,658
Third ....do.... 128,420

Total..do.... 1,173,142
Average number of pounds of sugar per ton of cane...... 135.9

The manufacturing data for the last four weeks of the season, while under chemical control, are given in full in the following table:

Table of manufacturing data for four weeks.

	Cane ground.	Sulphured juice.	Weight per gallon.	Weight of juice.	Sugar in sulphured juice.	Sugar in sulphured juice.
	Tons.	*Gallons.*	*Pounds.*	*Pounds.*	*Per cent.*	*Pounds.*
Fifth week	1,247	202,782	8.86	1,796,650	12.45	224,683
Sixth week	1,117	169,822	8.86	1,504,623	12.83	193,043
Seventh week ...	1,392	233,842	8.85	2,069,501	12.72	263,240
Eighth week.....	1,139	191,084	8.84	1,689,183	13.00	219,594
For four weeks.	4,895	797,530	....	7,059,957	....	900,560

Table of manufacturing data for four weeks—Continued.

	Sugar per ton of cane obtained in sulphured juice.	Sugar in per cent. of weight of cane obtained in sulphured juice.	Merchantable sugar made.	Merchantable sugar per ton of cane.	Molasses obtained.	Molasses per ton of cane.
	Pounds.		*Pounds.*	*Pounds.*	*Pounds.*	*Pounds.*
Fifth week	180.2	9.01	182,621	146.4	64,522	51.7
Sixth week	172.8	8.64	158,905	142.3	56,523	50.6
Seventh week ...	189.1	9.45	204,820	147.1	105,457	75.8
Eighth week	192.8	9.53	189,730	166.6	68,838	60.4
For four weeks.	184.0	9.20	736,076	150.4	295,240	60.3

The following table gives in detail the amount of sugar obtained in the three successive sugars, and in the molasses.

Table showing sugar recovered.

	Merchantable sugar.	Merchantable sugar per ton of cane.	Pure sucrose of 100 per cent. polarization.	Pure sucrose per ton of cane.	Pure sucrose in per cent. of the amount present in the sulphured juice.
Fifth week:	*Pounds.*	*Pounds.*	*Pounds.*	*Pounds.*	*Per cent.*
First sugar	102,648	82.3	101,077	81.0	44.99
Second sugar ..	60,085	48.2	58,462	46.9	26.02
Third sugar....	19,888	15.9	17,820	14.3	7.93
Molasses			17,834	14.3	7.93
Total	182,621	146.4	195,193	156.5	86.87
Sixth week:					
First sugar	93,599	83.8	91,540	81.9	47.42
Second sugar ..	56,526	50.6	55,056	49.3	28.52
Third sugar ...	8,780	7.9	7,937	7.1	4.11
Molasses......			23,310	20.9	12.07
Total	158,905	142.3	177,843	159.2	92.12
Seventh week:					
First sugar	127,625	91.7	125,910	90.4	47.83
Second sugar..	70,356	50.5	69,160	49.7	26.27
Third sugar ...	6,839	4.9	5,950	4.3	2.26
Molasses.......			40,791	29.3	15.49
Total	204,820	147.1	241,811	173.7	91.85
Eighth week:					
First sugar ...	133,234	11.7	131,768	115.7	60.00
Second sugar ..	35,396	31.1	34,865	30.6	15.88
Third sugar ...	21,100	18.5	19,632	16.7	8.67
Molasses			27,087	24.3	12.61
Total	189,730	166.6	213,352	187.3	97.16
For four weeks:					
First sugar	457,106	93.4	450,235	92.0	50.00
Second sugar ..	222,363	45.4	217,543	44.4	24.16
Third sugar ...	56,607	11.6	50,739	10.4	5.63
Molasses			109,622	22.4	12.17
Total	736,076	150.4	828,199	169.2	91.96

From the foregoing data the losses in manufacture after the sulphured juice were computed are embodied in the table which follows:

Table showing losses.

	Sucrose.	Sucrose per ton of cane.	Per cent. of sugar present in sulphured juice inverted.
Fifth week:	*Pounds.*	*Pounds.*	*Pounds.*
Total inversion	11,734	9.40	5.22
Mechanical losses including scums and press cake.	17,756	14.24	7.90
Total	29,490	23.64	13.14
Sixth week:			
Total inversion	4,031	3.60	2.09
Mechanical losses	11,169	10.00	5.78
Total	15,200	13.60	7.87
Seventh week:			
Total inversion	10,647	7.65	4.04
Mechanical losses	10,782	7.75	4.10
Total	21,429	15.40	8.14
Eighth week:			
Total inversion	3,981	3.50	1.81
Mechanical losses	2,261	1.98	1.03
Total	6,242	5.48	2.84
For four weeks:			
Total inversion	30,393	6.21	3.37
Mechanical losses	41,968	8.57	4.66
Total	72,361	14.78	8.03

From the above showing it will be seen that the total loss in manufacture during the four weeks was 72,361 pounds of pure sucrose of 100 per cent. polarization (equal to 73,735 pounds of sugar polarizing 98 per cent., or 14.78 pounds for each ton of cane. This total loss constituted 8.03 per cent. of the amount of sugar present in the sulphured juice, which was taken as a starting-point. Of the 8.03 per cent. of total loss 3.37 per cent., or about 42 per cent. of the whole, is charged to inversion in the different operations, and 4.66 per cent., or about 58 per cent. of the whole, is charged to other sources of loss, comprehended under the general head of "mechanical losses." No division of these losses could be made, on account of lack of data. Probably the principal source was in the scums and filter-press cake, the amount of which could not be ascertained with any degree of accuracy. In the first part of the season the loss from this source was particularly heavy, as the capacity of the presses was insufficient, and difficulty was experienced in getting a hard cake. During the last two weeks less trouble was had in this respect.

The loss by inversion has been divided up and apportioned to the different operations, as shown in the following table:

Table showing inversion.

	Sucrose inverted.	Sucrose inverted per ton of cane.	Sucrose inverted in per cent. of the sucrose in the sulphured juice.
Fifth week :	*Pounds.*	*Pounds.*	*Per cent.*
Between sulphured juice and sirup	1,733	1.39	.77
Between sirup and first massecuite ...:...	828	.66	.37
Between first massecuite and molasses...	9,173	7.35	4.08
Total	11,734	9.40	5.22
Sixth week :			
Between sulphured juice and sirup	2,718	2.43	1.41
Between sirup and first massecuite	1,313	1.17	.68
Between first massecuite and molasses...	....	....	....
Total	4,031	3.60	2.09
Seventh week :			
Between sulphured juice and sirup	3,525	2.53	1.33
Between sirup and first massecuite......	1,332	.96	.51
Between first massecuite and molasses...	5,790	4.16	2.20
Total	10,647	7.65	4.04
Eighth week:			
Between sulphured juice and sirup	2,820	2.48	1.28
Between sirup and first massecuite	230	.20	.11
Between first massecuite and molasses ..	931	.82	.42
Total	3,981	3.50	1.81
For four weeks :			
Between sulphured juice and sirup	10,796	2.20	1.20
Between sirup and first massecuite......	3,703	.76	.41
Between first massecuite and molasses...	15,894	3.25	1.76
Total	30,393	6.21	3.37

The summary of total inversion for the four weeks shows that 30,393 pounds were lost in this way, or 6.21 pounds for each ton of cane, constituting 3.37 per cent. of the original amount of sugar present in the sulphured juice. Of this 3.37 per cent., 1.2 per cent. was inverted in reducing the juice to sirup, .41 per cent. in boiling to first massecuite, and 1.76 per cent. in the subsequent operations. It will be noticed in the table that the amount of inversion and its distribution among the various operations varied greatly in different weeks. This is partly due to

EXPERIMENTS IN ACID AND NEUTRAL CLARIFICATION,

which were carried out upon the different weekly runs. During the fifth week the ordinary clarification was used, during the sixth week an attempt at neutral clarification was made, but it was not very carefully watched. In the seventh week's run the clarification was made decidedly acid, and considerable sulphur was used. The eighth week's run was made with neutral clarification, pains being taken to have the juice fully neutral or even slightly alkaline, and probably it was all worked in this condition, unless possibly a little may have escaped observation at night.

The accuracy of the comparison of the results obtained by the different clarifications is somewhat vitiated by difficulty in separating the molasses when the thirds were run off in the spring. Mr. Binnings found that twenty-two cars, twelve of which belonged to the sixth week and ten to the seventh, would not purge, and he was obliged to melt them all up and run them into molasses; in consequence the proportion of this molasses belonging to each week's run could only be ascertained by estimation, so that a considerable error may have been introduced in this way, and the results are far from being so reliable as I could have wished; such as they are, however, they show a great advantage in favor of the neutral clarification so far as the reduction in inversion and yield of sugar is concerned. This will be plainly apparent from an inspection of the tables. The least amount of inversion was during the eighth week, when a careful neutral clarification was insured, the difference between this and the preceding week, when the clarification was acid, being 4.1 lbs. per ton, or 2.23 per cent. of the sugar in the original juice. As the mechanical loss was also least in the eighth week, this run makes by far the best showing as to total losses, these being only 5.48 lbs. per ton, or 2.84 per cent. of the sugar in the juice. This shows what can be accomplished in the way of avoiding losses.

In the last table it will be seen that no inversion whatever is shown in the sixth week after the first massecuite. This anomalous result is doubtless due to the mixing up of the molasses between this week and the next, as explained above.

EXPERIMENTS BY SHORT RUNS.

The gain in yield of sugar obtained by neutral clarification was further investigated by several short runs, the sugar from which was kept separate. Of course these could not be followed through to the molasses, and the comparison is simply based upon the quantity of sugar obtained as compared with the available sugar in the juice, as shown by analysis. The available sugar is calculated by subtracting one and a half times the glucose from the sucrose present.

Table giving comparison of available sugar in juice, with actual yield in acid and neutral clarification.

Short run—	Clarifica-tion.	Cane.	Weight of juice.	Available sugar in juice.	Weight of available sugar in juice.	Pounds per ton available sugar in juice.
		Tons.	*Pounds.*	*Per cent.*	*Pounds.*	*Pounds.*
No. 1	Acid	239	375, 390	11. 70	43, 921	183. 7
No. 2	Neutral	209	278, 145	11. 28	31, 375	150. 1
No. 3	do	175	266, 339	11. 39	30. 336	173. 3

Short run—	Weight of mer-chantable sugar obtained 1sts, 2ds, and 3ds.	Pounds per ton mer-chantable sugar.	Weight of pure sucrose ob-tained.	Pounds per ton of pure sucrose.	Difference in pounds per ton be-tween pure sucrose ob-tained and available sugar in juice.
	Pounds.	*Pounds.*	*Pounds.*	*Pounds.*	*Pounds.*
No. 1	36, 833	154. 1	36, 152	151. 3	32. 4
No. 2	32, 060	153. 4	31, 401	150. 2	—. 1
No. 3	28, 719	164. 0	28, 209	161. 2	12. 1

There can be little doubt but that a neutral clarification greatly less-ens loss by inversion in the sugar house. Sugar made from a "heavy" clarification will not be quite so light in color, however, as where the juice is left slightly acid, and it is a question that still remains to be settled whether it is not more profitable to submit to some loss by in-version in order to improve the quality of the sugar. In our experi-ments the first and second sugar from juice clarified neutral was only a shade darker than that from acid juice, but the third sugar and molasses suffered more. Where the clarification is under chemical supervision and can be carefully watched, it may be best to use a slightly acid clarification, otherwise it is much safer to adhere to a neutral or even slightly alkaline clarification. The color of the juice is a very poor guide to go by, and the clarifier men should be trained to use test papers. A clarification that does not turn blue litmus paper red nor turmeric paper brown is a pretty safe neutral clarification.

LOSS BY INVERSION IN BOILING AND SKIMMING IN OPEN PAN.

From the table giving losses by inversion it will be seen that a con-siderable amount of inversion occurred in the operation of reducing the juice to sirup, and that this inversion persisted even through the neu-tral work of the eighth week. This was due partly to the boiling and skimming of the sirup in an open pan after it came from the double effect, and partly to same cause of inversion in the vacuum evaporator itself, which the limited time at my command did not allow me to in-vestigate. A series of experiments to ascertain the amount of inversion during the boiling in the open evaporator gave the following results:

Table showing effect of boiling and skimming in open evaporator.

	Before.					After.			
No.	Date.	Solids.	Sucrose.	Glucose.	No.	Date.	Solids.	Sucrose.	Glucose.
		Per cent.	Per cent.	Per cent.			Per cent.	Per cent.	Per cent.
13	Nov. 5	34.61	28.59	3.45	14	Nov. 5	35.61	29.38	3.65
24	Nov. 6	36.00	30.94	3.57	25	Nov. 6	38.70	32.50	3.85
33	Nov. 7	43.93	34.30	4.35	34	Nov. 7	44.77	35.10	4.67
43	Nov. 8	35.00	29.00	3.50	44	Nov. 8	36.00	29.90	3.73
59	Nov. 9	36.97	31.10	3.23	60	Nov. 9	38.37	32.10	3.57
69	Nov. 10	34.66	29.10	3.15	70	Nov. 10	35.56	29.80	3.23
Average....		36.86	30.50	3.54	Average....		38.17	31.43	3.78
Coefficient of purity.............				82.70	Coefficient of purity.............				82.39
Glucose per cent. sucrose........				11.57	Glucose per cent. sucrose........				12.63

Another series, made when neutral clarification was employed, gave the following results:

	Before.					After.			
No.	Date.	Solids.	Sucrose.	Glucose.	No.	Date.	Solids.	Sucrose.	Glucose.
		Per cent.	Per cent.	Per cent.			Per cent.	Per cent.	Per cent.
89	Nov. 13	....	36.70	3.50	90	Nov. 13	....	36.80	3.62
100	Nov. 14	34.99	30.00	2.84	101	Nov. 14	35.39	30.20	2.88
110	Nov. 15	43.47	35.80	2.95	111	Nov. 15	44.54	36.25	3.13
126	Nov. 16	39.67	33.80	2.87	127	Nov. 16	40.27	34.05	3.03
136	Nov. 17	44.47	38.35	3.01	137	Nov. 17	44.97	38.65	3.16
Average....		40.65	34.93	3.03	Average....		41.29	35.19	3.16
Coefficient of purity.............				85.90	Coefficient of purity.............				85.20
Guclose per cent. sucrose........				8.67	Glucose per cent. sucrose........				8.98

The first series shows an inversion of .39 per cent. of the sucrose present, and the second of .27 per cent. I could not be certain that the clarification was uniformly neutral during the second series.

The inversion produced by boiling and skimming sirup in an open evaporator was investigated by Mr. Spencer and myself at Magnolia, in 1884, and the results are given in Bulletin No. 5, p. 55. It seems strange that planters should adhere to this practice. The analyses above show that the purity is diminished instead of increased by the operation, so the idea that the sirup is improved by skimming off the foam which forms upon it is a delusion. None but insoluble substances could possibly be removed in this way, and they would be much more easily and effectually removed by settling. The heat required to bring the sirup to a boil is entirely wasted, unless it is taken into the strike-pan immediately, which is seldom the case. In the operation as performed at Des Lignes the sirup was subjected but a short time to a high heat, being merely brought to a boil and skimmed once or twice Still the inversion was appreciable, and when the operation is prolonged it is easy to see that a very considerable inversion might result. This operation will be entirely dispensed with at Des Lignes next season.

EFFECT OF HEATING SULPHURED JUICES BEFORE THE ADDITION OF LIME.

As I have previously indicated, the sulphured juice was taken as a starting point in the control work, as this was the first point where an accurate gauging and sampling of the juice could be obtained. Losses prior to this point, therefore, do not appear in the above showing. The operation of sulphuring was carefully watched, however, and means taken to insure a pretty thorough washing of the sulphur fumes.[1] I do not think the loss was very large in this operation.

A few analyses were made to determine the extent of inversion produced by heating the sulphured juice before the addition of lime. The results are given in the following table. The samples are strictly comparable, being taken from the same clarifierful of juice, the first while cold, and the second after heating the juice to a boil before the addition of lime.

Table showing effect of heating sulphured juice before the addition of lime.

	Before heating.					After heating.			
No.	Date.	Solids.	Sucrose.	Glucose.	No.	Date.	Solids.	Sucrose.	Glucose.
		Per cent.	Per cent.	Per cent.			Per cent.	Per cent.	Per cent.
105	Nov. 15	15.18	12.43	1.96	106	Nov. 15	14.81	12.60	1.10
123	Nov. 16	15.61	13.49	.93	124	Nov. 16	15.57	13.44	.97
133	Nov. 17	15.50	13.35	.95	134	Nov. 17	15.94	13.44	.99
144	Nov. 19	15.20	12.83	1.10	145	Nov. 19	15.24	12.97	1.11
151	Nov. 19	15.06	12.49	1.16	152	Nov. 19	15.10	12.59	1.18
158	Nov. 20	14.64	12.51	1.00	159	Nov. 20	14.84	12.50	1.03
164	Nov. 20	14.80	12.70	.99	165	Nov. 20	14.74	12.55	.99
172	Nov. 21	14.76	12.59	.93	173	Nov. 21	14.91	12.73	.95
182	Nov. 22	14.58	12.31	1.00	183	Nov. 22	14.81	12.44	1.02
189	Nov. 22	14.66	12.99	.90	190	Nov. 22	14.74	12.80	.89
196	Nov. 23	14.94	13.03	.89	197	Nov. 23	14.91	13.00	.89
203	Nov. 23	14.88	12.74	.91	204	Nov. 23	14.88	12.69	.93
206	Nov. 24	14.96	13.22	.80	207	Nov. 24	15.10	13.11	.84
213	Nov. 24	14.44	12.47	.82	214	Nov. 24	14.41	12.51	.84
Average....		14.94	12.80	.96	Average....		14.98	12.82	.98
Coefficient of purity.......				85.70	Coefficient of purity.............				85.60
Glucose per cent. sucrose				7.50	Glucose per cent. sucrose				7.64

The inversion is very slight, being only .12 per cent. of the sugar present, but as it seems just as effective to add the lime before heating,

---

[1] The method of washing sulphur fumes employed at Des Lignes was described by Mr. Shattuck in a meeting of the Cane Growers' Association, and can be found on page 236, vol. I, of the Louisiana Planter.

even this inversion is probably unnecessary. Liming the cold juice before heating was practiced throughout the season, the exceptions above being simply for purposes of experiment.

A plan devised by Mr. Studniczka for preventing inversion by sulphuring was in use during part of the season. It consisted in adding carbonate of lime (whiting) to the sulphured juice, the object being to neutralize any sulphuric acid which might be brought into the juice from defective washing of the fumes. The method of application is fully described in the issue of the Planter cited above. Lack of time and the difficulty of obtaining comparable samples prevented my investigating its merits very closely. The quantity of whiting required, and the labor involved in keeping it in operation, caused its discontinuance during the greater part of the season. It would doubtless prove very useful in case of defective washing arrangements, but can hardly be considered better than the addition of a small quantity of milk of lime to the juice before sulphuring, which Professor Becnel[1] found very effectual in the work at Belle Alliance. The only advantage the carbonate would possess over the hydrate of lime would be in the fact that an excess could be added without danger of rendering the juice alkaline.

FUEL CONSUMPTION.

The amount of coal consumed during the season was 486 tons 1,284 pounds. The quantity used in running off the thirds was estimated, and the whole consumption placed at 555 tons. This gives the fuel consumption, exclusive of bagasse, as follows:

Pounds of coal per 1,000 pounds sugar......................... 946
Pounds of coal per ton of cane................................ 128

No wood was used except to start the bagasse furnace.

EXPERIMENTS IN MACERATION BETWEEN MILLS.

The method of maceration by means of the addition of hot water or steam to the cane, or to the bagasse between mills, where supplemental mills are employed, is quite an old practice. It is largely used in Cuba and the Hawaiian Islands, and has often been employed in Louisiana. In common with many other methods in cane work, however, it seems to have been applied in a blind, empirical, and careless manner, and I can find no record of any careful study having been made as to the best methods of application, the limits of its usefulness, or its effect upon the quality of the juices obtained.

I found it in operation at Des Lignes upon my arrival, and proceeded to make some little observation and experiment as to its efficiency, though it will readily be understood from the very limited time I had that the study I was able to make was of a very superficial character.

---

[1] Report on the results of Belle Alliance, Evan Hall, and Souvenir sugar-houses for the crop of 1888, p. 8, New Orleans, 1889.

Some of the results are very unsatisfactory and conflicting, owing to difficulty in controlling the conditions, but I will insert them notwithstanding, hoping that they will at least serve to call attention to the method and secure it a wider application in mill work the coming season, and closer and more careful study.

The water was added at Des Lignes by means of a rectangular tin box with the bottom pierced full of holes so as to serve as a rose; this box was about 8 inches wide, and in length somewhat less than the width of the intermediate carrier, over which it was hung. It was connected with an exhaust receiver, and a valve placed just above the rose served to regulate the flow of the hot water through the latter. Probably a better method of application is that used by Mr. Thompson at Calumet, which will be found described in Mr. Edson's report.

The amount of water added at Des Lignes was not subject to any careful regulation. The pressure of the exhaust receiver caused variations in the supply of water, and it was necessary to set the valve in the pipe leading to the rose to correspond; then the perforations in the latter would become clogged at times, and this would hinder the flow, so that altogether the supply was quite irregular. The general idea followed was to give the bagasse about all the water it would absorb. It was surprising to see how much water would be taken up in this way without dripping from the carrier. The quantity of water which passed through the fine perforations of the rose was not fully appreciated until it was collected by running it off in a trough for a certain length of time and weighing the amount obtained.

The following results of experiments of this kind made at different times during the season show the amount of water added during a certain time, and indicate the variation in the supply at different periods. The quantities are all calculated to a period of one hour, though the actual time during which the water was collected was in some cases a shorter and in some a longer period:

	Lbs	Galls.
First experiment, November 13	1,818 or	218
Second experiment, November 14	1,500	180
Third experiment, November 16	1,356	163
Fourth experiment, November 24	1,776	213
Fifth experiment, November 30	2,622	315

The last trial given was made in connection with an experiment to be described later on, in which an extra quantity of water was used; omitting this, the average of four trials gives 1,612 pounds or 193 gallons of water added in an hour. The average quantity of cane ground per hour was about 10 tons. Taking the extraction of the mills without water as being 68 per cent., this would be a dilution of about 12 per cent. This is a rough estimate, of course, and a better basis of calculation is afforded by the following table, giving the results of comparative analyses of juices from the mill with and without water. The samples

for these analyses were taken as carefully as possible, first with the
maceration water turned on just as the mill was being run out at the
time; then the rose was turned off, and after sufficient time had elapsed
for the displacement of the diluted juice by the normal, samples were
taken as before. The sample of first mill juice was taken simply as a
matter of comparison, of course, it being unaffected by the dilution.
The second mill juices were taken only during the latter half of the
three weeks covered by the samples.

Table of analyses of normal and maceration juices.

	No.	Date.	Solids.	Sucrose.	Glucose.
			Per cent.	*Per cent.*	*Per cent.*
Mixed juice, without water....	67	Nov. 10	15.87	13.75	1.06
	82	Nov. 13	15.30	12.85	1.26
	87	Nov. 13	15.58	12.90	1.33
	92	Nov. 14	15.76	13.37	1.23
	102	Nov. 15	16.07	13.78	1.09
	122	Nov. 16	15.53	13.57	1.08
	132	Nov. 17	16.20	14.32	.91
	140	Nov. 17	15.87	13.82	.94
	143	Nov. 19	16.01	13.71	1.20
	155	Nov. 20	15.50	13.37	1.12
	169	Nov. 21	15.20	13.24	.98
	179	Nov. 22	15.50	13.08	1.02
	193	Nov. 23	15.47	13.67	.86
	218	Nov. 26	15.90	13.98	.93
	239	Nov. 27	15.37	13.62	.87
	257	Nov. 28	15.76	13.98	.81
	273	Nov. 29	16.01	14.36	.71
	295	Nov. 30	16.37	14.74	.59
Average..........			15.74	13.67	1.00
Coefficient of purity...........					86.85
Glucose per 100 sucrose........					7.31
Mixed juice, diluted...........	66	Nov. 10	14.37	12.21	1.13
	81	Nov. 13	14.06	11.74	1.09
	86	Nov. 13	14.48	12.17	1.30
	91	Nov. 14	14.66	12.39	1.16
	103	Nov. 15	14.90	12.72	1.05
	120	Nov. 16	14.53	12.64	1.10
	130	Nov. 17	15.00	13.16	1.02
	138	Nov. 17	15.56	13.45	1.00
	141	Nov. 19	14.91	12.93	1.02
	153	Nov. 20	14.34	12.25	1.05
	167	Nov. 21	14.30	12.16	.93
	177	Nov. 22	14.20	12.31	.90
	191	Nov. 23	14.80	12.97	.93
	216	Nov. 26	15.23	13.34	.85
	237	Nov. 27	15.07	13.10	.83
	255	Nov. 28	15.01	13.19	.89
	271	Nov. 29	14.61	13.07	.67
	293	Nov. 30	15.00	13.35	.56
Average..........			14.72	12.75	.97
Coefficient of purity...........					86.62
Glucose per 100 sucrose					7.61

Table of analyses of normal and maceration juices—Continued.

	No.	Date.	Solids.	Sucrose.	Glucose.
			Per cent.	Per cent.	Per cent.
First mill juice only	83	Nov. 13	15.70	13.17	1.44
	88	Nov. 13	15.81	13.23	1.47
	93	Nov. 14	16.30	13.78	1.27
	104	Nov. 15	16.57	14.73	1.01
	121	Nov. 16	16.50	14.64	1.05
	131	Nov. 17	16.51	14.59	1.09
	139	Nov. 17	16.77	14.89	1.05
	142	Nov. 19	16.41	14.26	1.22
	154	Nov. 20	16.60	14.43	1.00
	168	Nov. 21	16.60	14.63	1.00
	178	Nov. 22	15.80	13.65	1.04
	192	Nov. 2?	16.07	13.98	1.03
	217	Nov. 26	16.50	14.53	1.00
	238	Nov. 27	16.03	13.93	.98
	256	Nov. 28	16.01	14.36	.91
	272	Nov. 29	16.36	14.93	.79
	294	Nov. 30	16.90	15.09	.61
Average	......	....	16.32	14.23	1.06
Coefficient of purity	......	....	....	....	87.50
Glucose per 100 sucrose	......	....	....	....	7.63
Second mill juice without water	157	Nov. 20	14.36	11.97	.88
	171	Nov. 21	13.54	11.52	.80
	181	Nov. 22	13.82	11.59	.91
	195	Nov. 23	14.22	12.17	.76
	220	Nov. 26	14.67	12.53	.71
	241	Nov. 27	15.13	13.05	.77
	259	Nov. 28	13.40	11.51	.67
	275	Nov. 29	14.97	12.81	.79
	297	Nov. 30	15.23	13.29	.43
Average	......	....	14.37	12.27	.75
Coefficient of purity...........	......	....	....	....	85.39
Glucose per 100 sucrose........	......	....	....	....	6.11
Second mill juice, dilated	156	Nov. 20	11.56	9.76	.72
	170	Nov. 21	11.10	9.68	.63
	180	Nov. 22	11.04	9.33	.62
	194	Nov. 23	11.31	9.70	.57
	219	Nov. 26	11.73	10.25	.63
	240	Nov. 27	10.61	9.04	.53
	258	Nov. 28	10.50	9.14	.52
	274	Nov. 29	11.50	10.01	.48
	296	Nov. 30	10.53	9.25	.35
Average	......	....	11. 0	9.57	.56
Coefficient of purity	......	....	....	....	86.21
Glucose per 100 sucrose........	......	....	....	....	5.85

From the averages of the diluted and undiluted mixed juices given in this table the dilution is seen to be :

	Per cent.
Calculated upon the per cent. of total solids......................	6.93
Calculated upon the per cent. of total sucrose...................	7.22

The dilution of the second mill juice is :

Per cent.

Calculated upon the per cent. of total solids..................... 29. 46

Calculated upon the per cent. of total sucrose.................... 28. 21

The increased extraction brought about by this dilution can not be accurately estimated, but some approximation to it may be made.

Comparing the amount of sugar in the juice as shown by these samples (see table on p 15) with the amount in the sulphured juice we have the following data for the three weeks during which samples of the undiluted juices were taken :

	Sugar in cane.	Sugar in sulphured juice.	Extraction on weight of juice.
	Pounds.	*Pounds.*	*Per cent.*
Sixth week ...	275, 854	193, 043	69. 98
Seventh week.	342, 014	263, 240	76. 97
Eighth week .	289, 898	219, 594	75. 74
Average extraction for three weeks......			74. 23

This would be only 66.81 per cent. of the weight of cane, which seems pretty low. The basis of calculation is rather unfavorable to the extraction, of course, as all juice lost between the mill and the sulphured juices counts against the extraction. Two or three tests of extraction were made during the season by running through a weighed quantity of cane without adding water. These gave results ranging from 64 to 68 per cent. of the weight of cane. Probably the most reliable data in regard to the increased yield of sugar from maceration are furnished by the results of a single

SPECIAL EXPERIMENT

which was carried through upon a uniform lot of cane, all taken from the same cut. A weighed portion of this cane was run through the mill without water, the juice all collected in gauged tanks, and an accurate sample obtained of the whole body of juice. Another weighed portion of the same cane was then run through in a similar manner, except that the maceration water was turned on. An accurate estimate of the quantity of sugar obtained in each case was furnished by the analysis, and the analysis of the juice which was run through without water gave a basis for the calculation of the quantity of sugar in the cane used for both runs, upon the presumption that the cane was of uniform quality. The results were as follows:

Table giving results of special experiment in maceration.

	Without maceration.	With maceration.
Pounds of cane ground	18,060	14,800
Gallons of juice obtained	1,416	1,358
Pounds of juice obtained..	12,588	12,032
Pounds sucrose obtained..	1,855.5	1,606.3
Pounds sucrose obtained per ton of cane	205.5	217.1
Difference in favor of maceration in pounds per ton	....	11.6
Sucrose obtained per cent. of cane..............................	10.27	10.85
Difference in favor of maceration per cent. of cane	....	.58
Per cent. extraction on weight of juice	77.35	81.81
Per cent. extraction on weight of cane........................	69.61	73.61
Difference in favor of maceration per cent. extraction........	....	4.00

The amount of water added was greater than the average used during the season, and was about all the cane could be made to absorb, with the conditions under which the water was added.

The analyses of the juices gave the following figures:

	Without maceration.	With maceration.
Solids ....per cent..	16.37	15.00
Sucrose ....do....	14.74	13.35
Glucose ....do....	.59	.56
Co-efficient of purity....................	90.00	89.00
Glucose per hundred sucrose	4.00	4.19

Samples of second mill juices were taken during the runs, which gave the following:

	Without maceration.	With maceration.
Solids......................per cent ..	15.23	10.53
Sucrose ....do	13.29	9.25
Glucose........................do	.43	.35
Co-efficient of purity..................	87.20	87.84
Glucose per hundred sucrose	3.23	3.78

From the above the dilution is seen to be—

	Per cent.
Calculated on the solids.................................	9.13
Calculated on the sucrose..............................	10.41

The dilution of the second mill juice is—

	Per cent.
Calculated on the solids	44.64
Calculated on the sucrose..............................	42.60

A set of samples was obtained of Colonel Dulroca, manager of Mr. Cartwright Eustis's Fusilier plantation, who practiced maceration during the season, and analyzed with the following results:

Analyses of maceration juices from Fusilier plantation.

	Mixed juice without water.	Mixed juice with water.	First juice only.
Solids ....per cent..	15.33	12.83	16.63
Sucrose..................... do....	13.48	11.39	14.87
Glucose..................... do....	.93	.71	.82
Co-efficient purity	87.28	88.78	89.40
Glucose per hundred sucrose	6.90	6.23	5.51

These analyses show a much greater dilution than any taken at Des Lignes, as follows:

Per cent.

Calculated on the solids............................... 19.48

Calculated on the sucrose 18.35

At my request Colonel Dulroca made a test to ascertain the amount of water he was using, and found it to be 4,350 pounds, or 522 gallons, per hour. He did not know how much better extraction he was getting with this water, but was quite certain it was considerable.

QUALITY OF JUICES.

The series of analyses given in the table on page 25 shows the average co-efficient of purity of the mixed juices with maceration to be .23 lower than the corresponding mixed juices without water. The juices in the special experiment showed (page 28) a difference of 1 in the same direction. Colonel Dulroca's juices, on the other hand, show a difference of 1.5 in the opposite direction. Of course I could not tell how these latter juices were taken, as they were sent to me. A very singular thing about the series of analyses, which I am able to account for only by imperfect sampling, is that the analyses of the second mill juices show a higher purity in those taken with water than without in every case except one. In view of the fact that the mixed juices, even taking the average of those corresponding to these samples of second mill juice, show a lower co-efficient in the diluted juice, and as this could only be brought about by a deterioration of the second mill juice I am forced to the conclusion that the samples were not comparable. The samples of mixed juices, being taken from a receptacle, are more reliable than those of the single mills, which had to be taken from a spout at intervals. In beet work it has been shown to be the case that juices obtained by maceration are always less pure than by simple pressure.

The use of "continuous presses" (in contradistinction to hydraulic presses, which operate intermittingly) in beet work, with the addition of water to the pulp, furnishes an interesting parallel to the use of double milling with maceration between the mills, and I would advise any one who desired to make a study of the matter to consult the German and French authorities on "double pressure." A few years ago it was held by many, especially in France, that diffusion would never supplant the use of continuous presses with maceration. Time has shown them to be wrong in this, however, and diffusion is conceded to be the method par excellence for juice extraction by the entire sugar-making world.

But there is no doubt whatever that double milling with maceration could be made as superior to the old method of single milling in cane work as the continuous presses with maceration have been shown to be superior to the method of single pressure in a hydraulic press with beets. In beet work the maceration is carried much further than in the simple method used in cane, which is not properly maceration but *saturation.* Water is added not only between the two pressings, but also to the first pulp before the first pressing. The quantity of water added is from 40 to 50 per cent. of the weight of the beets, and macerating machines are used to tear up the pulp between the presses and mix it with the maceration water.

According to Stammer,[1] the method which has given the best results is to return the dilute juice from the second pressing to the fresh pulp, the water being added between the presses. This might be possible with cane in connection with shredding. It seems hardly necessary or advisable to go into the refinements of the method of maceration in the effort to adapt them to cane work, in view of the fact that improvements in this line have been abandoned for the better method of diffusion. Considering it simply as a make shift, therefore, as Mr. Thompson calls it in his letter to Mr. Wilkinson on this subject,[2] the question is how best to use it in connection with the present mill plants, until such time as these can be exchanged for the diffusion battery. There can be no doubt whatever of its efficiency, even in the crude and simple manner in which it is now applied.

The experiments at Calumet, which will be described in Mr. Edson's report, were much more thorough and conclusive than mine, and the results are equally favorable to maceration. This was doubtless a season in which it was particularly applicable, on account of the hard and woody nature of the cane; but still the conclusion can be drawn with tolerable certainty that the extraction of a double mill can be increased fully 5 per cent. with a dilution of only 10 per cent , by simply sprinkling the intermediate carrier with water. The simplicity of the matter is more apparent than real, however; for if it were desired to regulate it carefully, and adjust dilution to extraction so as to attain the most economical results, it would be found more difficult to gauge and con-

---

[1] Lehrbuch der Zuckerfabrikation, vol. 1

[2] "The Diffusion Process," pamphlet by J. B. Wilkinson. New Orleans, 1889, page 54.

, trol than diffusion, owing to the empirical conditions under which it is applied.

The amount of water added is not known ; the amount of bagasse to which it is added is not known, and there is no way of ascertaining even approximately the amount of dilution, except by turning off the water and comparing the juices. No hard and fast rule can be laid down as to gauging the dilution by comparison of the first and second mill juices with the water running, as much depends upon the relative extraction of the two mills. According to Mr. Young,[1] in the method as used on the Waiakea plantation, Hawaiian Islands, the dilution is carried to such an extent that the juice from the supplemental mill stands one-fourth to one-third the density of that from the first mill. It will be seen that this indicates a much greater dilution than the work at Calumet or Des Lignes, and I hardly see how it would be possible to attain it by simply sprinkling the carrier, which seems to have been the method he employed.

For a careful study of the operation some means of knowing the amount of water added is very desirable. Doubtless the work at Calumet the coming season will throw much more light upon the matter than we have at present.

EXPERIMENTS SHOWING IMPROVEMENT IN CANE BY STANDING AND RIPENING.

The mill was set in operation entirely too early in the season this year. The crop was over-estimated, as it was almost universally this season, and with the limited capacity of the house it was feared that if the campaign was not opened early it would not be able to handle it before freezing weather set in. Planters often have this problem presented to them. It is a matter of choice between two evils, whether to work green cane on the one hand or to run the chance of an early freeze on the other. Perhaps the extent of the former evil may not be fully appreciated, however, and in this connection a few experiments made with a view to ascertain the improvement that can be made by standing cane towards the end of the season may prove of interest.

On four different cuts a portion of the cane was left uncut and allowed to stand until the last day of the campaign, when it was run through the mill ; a sample of the juice obtained was submitted to analysis, and compared with the juice from the same cane at the first cutting. The number of comparisons was not great, but the conditions of comparison were fairly good, as a considerable quantity of cane was left for the second sample, enough to fill several carts, and the samples of juice represented the entire body of cane pretty well, being obtained in a manner I have already described elsewhere.[1] The results of the analysis may be relied on as giving accurately the relative composition

[1] The Planters' Monthly, vol. 8, 1889, p. 179.
[1] Louisiana Planter, June 15, 1889.

of the juice at the two periods; they are given in the following table, together with the length of time the cane was allowed to stand. The available sugar is calculated upon the formula of sucrose minus one and one-half times the glucose:

Table showing improvement in cane by ripening.

STORE CUT.

Date of analysis	Solids	Sucrose	Glucose	Co effi cient of purity	Available sugar in juice.	Pounds per ton availa ble sugar, at 70 per cent ex- traction	Differ- ence.
	Per cent	*Per cent*	*Per cent*		*Per cent*	*Pounds*	*Pounds*
Nov. 14	15 46	13 34	1 09	86 3	11 74	163 8	... ...
Nov. 30	15 83	13 99	88	88 4	12 67	177 4	13 6

Average improvement per day in pounds per ton, .85

BOYLE CUT

Nov 17	15 87	13.82	94	87 1	12 41	173 7	....
Nov. 30	16. 47	14 88	.66	90 3	13 89	194.5	20 8

Average improvement per day in pounds per ton, 1 6.

CLARA CUT.

Nov 19	15 94	13 80	1 01	86 6	12 28	171 9	....
Nov 30	16 23	14 75	53	90 9	13 95	195 3	23 4

Average improvement per day in pounds per ton, 2.13

SILLAN CUT

Nov 21	14 80	12 97	.96	87 6	11 53	161 4	....
Nov 30	15 77	13 80	.81	87 9	12 63	176 8	15. 4

Average improvement per day in pounds per ton, 1 71.
Average improvement per day in pounds per ton for all four cuts, 1 56.

It will be seen that the improvement in the juice was remarkable in every case, although the longest period allowed to elapse between the first and second analyses was only sixteen days. The per cent. of sucrose, and the purity coefficient are greatly increased, and the per cent. of glucose diminished. Calculated out in a practical way to show the increase in available sugar which would be obtained at 70 per cent. extraction, one plat shows as high as 23 pounds per ton for a period of eleven days. With a greater extraction the increase would be much more. The average increase of the four plats is 1.56 pounds of available sugar per ton for *each day* the cane was allowed to stand. Thus, a crop of 10,000 tons would improve at the rate of 15,600 pounds per day of pure sucrose, equal to at least 16,500 pounds of merchantable sugar, so that two weeks would add nearly a quarter of a million pounds to the amount of sugar that could be actually obtained from it.

FERTILIZATION.

Quite a number of analyses were made at the request of the proprietors of the plantation from cuts of cane that had been differently fertilized with the end in view of determining the relative value of the fertilizers used. As no precautions had been taken to secure uniformity of conditions in other respects, however, I could attach little importance to the results, and will not reproduce them here. Such experiments are valuable only when carried out with the greatest care as regards the conditions of comparison, and even then great discrimination of judgment is required in arriving at conclusions from a careful balancing of results.

ADOPTION OF DIFFUSION FOR THE COMING CAMPAIGN AT DES LIGNES

Messrs. Shattuck & Hoffman have become so much impressed with the advantages of the diffusion method for the extraction of juice, as shown by the experiments of the Department, and were so thoroughly convinced of its superiority over milling by its successful operation at Governor Warmoth's and Colonel Cunningham's last season, that they have decided to adopt it at Des Lignes for this year's campaign. As this bulletin goes to press a double-line battery, with an estimated capacity of 400 tons a day, is in process of erection at the plantation, supplemented by greatly increased evaporating facilities, and great pains are being taken to have the equipment of the house complete in all respects. Contracts have been made with neighboring planters for their crops of cane, and it is expected that a considerable amount will be worked up. In view of the size of the plant, and of the advantage which would be derived by the industry from a careful control and study of the season's work, arrangements have been made whereby the Department will have control of the chemical work, and a complete report of the season's operations will be made after the close of the campaign.

7082—Bull. 22——3

INDEX.

Lightning Source UK Ltd.
Milton Keynes UK
UKOW02f1840031013

218459UK00009B/532/P